DOGS SET III

Pugs

Bob Temple

ABDO Publishing Company

visit us at
www.abdopub.com

Published by ABDO Publishing Company, 4940 Viking Drive, Suite 622, Edina, Minnesota 55435.

Printed in the United States.

Edited by: Paul Joseph

Photo credits: Peter Arnold, Inc.; Ron Kimball Photography

Library of Congress Cataloging-in-Publication Data

Temple, Bob.
     Pugs / Bob Temple
           p. cm. — (Dogs. Set III)
     ISBN 1-57765-422-6
     1. Pug—Juvenile literature. [1. Pug. 2. Dogs. 3. Pets] I. Title.

SF429.P9 T36 2000
636.76—dc21
                    00-036190

Contents

Where Dogs Come From

Dogs have been living with humans for thousands of years. Millions of dogs are family pets. Some dogs are workers who help farmers herd their sheep. Other dogs help hunters out in the fields.

You may have heard dogs being called "canines." This is because they are from the species called Canidae, from the Latin word canis, which means "dog."

There are other members of this family of animals that live in the wild. Wolves, foxes, and wild dogs are all related in some way to the dogs that we have as pets!

Opposite page: The Pug, like all dogs, is related to the wolf.

Pugs

Pugs are from the "toy" group of dogs. They are very small, with short, smooth hair, and a wrinkled, pushed-in face. The Pug's motto is "multum in parvo," which means "a lot of dog in a little body."

Its thick chest and fighter's stance make the Pug look like it is always ready for action. The Pug also has a lot of heart and a very big bark!

The Pug is one of the oldest **breeds** of dogs. It started in China and Tibet more than 2,400 years ago.

In the 16th century, the Pug became the mascot for the country of Holland, after the prince's Pug licked his face and barked to warn him that the Spanish army was invading. The Pug nearly became extinct in later years, but since it was brought to America, it has been increasing in popularity.

Opposite page: The Pug started over 2,000 years ago in China.

What They're Like

Pugs are happy little dogs that love to be in the middle of the action. They are very friendly and love to play with people.

Pugs are smart and easy to train. Some times, they shy away from babies, but they get along great with children.

Pugs also like to be with other dogs, especially other Pugs. Many Pug owners have two or more of them.

Most Pugs live indoors with their human families. They like to play outside, but not when it's too hot or too cold. They like to go on walks with their owners.

Pugs are very friendly and love to be with people.

Coat and Color

A Pug's **coat** is made up of short, thin fur that is very soft and smooth. It usually doesn't need to be trimmed, unless your Pug is a show dog.

The Pug's face and ears are black, and its body can be black, silver, or apricot.

The lighter-colored Pugs have a black line of fur that runs straight down their backs from their necks to their tails. Their tails are short and curled up tight on their backs.

Opposite page: Pugs are usually black but can also be silver or apricot.

After about four weeks, you can begin to feed them soft puppy food. At this time, they need less and less of their mother's milk. This is called weaning.

Pug puppies need a nice, warm place to rest.

Glossary

breed: a group of dogs that share the same appearance and characteristics.

coat: the hair that covers a dog's body.

diet: the food that your dog eats.

distemper: a contagious disease that dogs sometimes get. It is caused by a virus.

license (LIE-sense): a tag worn by a dog indicating it has been registered with a city.

litter: the group of puppies a dog has in one pregnancy.

mammal: warm-blooded animals that feed their babies milk from the mother's body.

nutrition (new-TRISH-un): food; nourishment.

pregnant: with one or more babies growing within the body.

rabies: a dangerous disease that dogs can get.

veterinarian (VET-er-in-AIR-ian): your dog's doctor; also called a vet.

Internet Sites

PugZone

www.pugzone.com

This site is full of Pug features, including how to get ready for your Pug before you bring him home. You can find Pug care tips, information on breeders, and how to train your Pug. You can also learn how to get into showing your Pug.

The American Kennel Club

http://www.akc.org

Information about many breeds, including the Pug. This page includes physical characteristics and a great deal about its history. You can also find breeder information. There is a message board for Pug owners to exchange information.

Index

Size

Pugs are toy dogs, but they are one of the bigger toy **breeds**. They usually weigh between 14 and 18 pounds (6.4 to 8.2 kg). They stand 10 or 11 inches (25 to 28 cm) high at the shoulder.

Their faces are round and deeply wrinkled. They have big, round eyes that sparkle when they are excited. Their ears are short and soft, and they point down. Their nose is very short, and it makes the Pug look like its face has been pushed in.

Opposite page: The Pug's face is round and wrinkled.

Care

Like most dogs, Pugs love attention. They want to be played with and to be a part of the family. But they also need care.

A Pug needs to be brushed at least twice a week to keep its **coat** and skin healthy. Since Pugs also tend to shed their fur, brushing will help keep hair from getting all over the house. They only need a bath every two weeks or so, but their eyes should be gently washed every other day.

Pugs need to be walked at least once a day to keep them in good shape. Because of their pushed-in face, Pugs sometimes have breathing problems, especially in hot weather.

Like all dogs, Pugs need to get shots from the **vet** every year. These shots help keep them from getting diseases like **distemper**.

Pugs also need lots of love. A period of time every day in which a Pug can curl up next to a family member also helps keep them happy and healthy.

Pugs love to be held.

Feeding

Good **nutrition** is important for every dog. Without the right food, your Pug won't be a happy, healthy member of the family.

When you first get a puppy, you should feed it the same food it has been eating. Puppies need to eat four or five small meals each day. As they get older, fewer feedings are required. For most adult dogs, one feeding per day is enough.

Make sure your Pug is getting a well-balanced **diet**. Your dog's **veterinarian** can help you decide what food is best. Once you have found the right food, you shouldn't change it. Changing the type of food you give your dog can upset their stomach and make them sick. Always make sure there is plenty of clean, fresh water for your dog to drink.

Opposite page: Pugs need a proper diet to stay healthy and happy.

Things They Need

Even though Pugs love to be in the middle of the action, they also need a quiet place to rest. A dog bed or a blanket that is placed in a quiet spot in the house will help your Pug get the sleep it needs. You'll know when your Pug is asleep, because they tend to snore!

Pugs should live indoors, but they also need plenty of outdoor exercise. A good walk or a game of fetch will help your Pug stay fit. A few dog toys like a ball or a bone can be kept in the house for indoor play.

Every dog should have a collar with a tag that includes the owner's name, address, and telephone number. This way, if the dog gets lost, the owner can be called. In most cities, dogs also need a **license**. And most dogs wear a tag that says they have gotten their **rabies** shot.

In order to be a good member of the family, your dog needs to be trained. Most dogs are happy to learn how to please their owners.

Pugs have a lot of energy and need to be exercised.

Puppies

Pugs can have as many as five puppies in a **litter**. Sometimes, only two puppies are born. Pugs are usually **pregnant** for about two months before they have their puppies. If you find out your Pug is pregnant, give her a sturdy box in a dark, warm place in the house. Put a blanket in the box for her. This is where she will have her puppies. Make sure to get lots of advice from your **veterinarian** if your Pug is pregnant.

Pug puppies are very helpless when they are born. All dogs are **mammals**, which means they drink milk from their mother's body when they are newborns. Because of the Pug's short nose, feeding is sometimes difficult for Pug puppies. Their noses get pressed up against their mother's body, making it hard for them to breathe.